Okanagan College
Curriculum Resource Centre

Amazing Monkeys

WRITTEN BY
SCOTT STEEDMAN

PHOTOGRAPHED BY
JERRY YOUNG

Stoddart

Conceived and produced by
Dorling Kindersley Limited

Project editor Christine Webb
Art editor Ann Cannings
Senior art editor Jacquie Gulliver
Production Louise Barratt

Illustrations by Gill Elsbury and Julie Anderson
Animals supplied by Trevor Smith's Animal World
Editorial consultants The staff of the Natural History Museum, London

The author would like to dedicate this book to Al and Joss.

Published in Canada in 1991 by Stoddart Publishing Co. Limited
34 Lesmill Road, Toronto, Canada M3B 2T6
Published in Great Britain in 1991 by Dorling Kindersley Limited
9 Henrietta Street, London, England WC2E 8PS

Canadian Cataloguing in Publication Data
Steedman, Scott

Amazing monkeys

(Amazing worlds)

ISBN 0-7737-2472-9

1. Monkeys - Juvenile literature. I. Young, Jerry. II. Title.

III. Series.
QL737.P9S86 1991   j599.8'2   C90-095673-9

Color reproduction by Colourscan, Singapore
Typeset by Windsorgraphics, Ringwood, Hampshire
Printed in Italy by A. Mondadori Editore, Verona

Contents

What is a monkey?

Monkeys and apes are our closest relatives. With its big eyes and clever face, this capuchin monkey looks surprisingly human. Most amazing of all are its hands – it has delicate fingers and thumbs just like ours.

Boy   Chimpanzee   Loris   Lemur

The monkey family
You belong to a group of animals called primates. So do apes (including chimps) and monkeys. The only other primates are the lemurs, which look like monkeys with foxy faces, and a few tiny night animals like the loris.

Look while you leap
Leaping through the trees is a dangerous business. Monkeys and apes have big eyes which face forward, making sure they can always spy a safe landing spot *before* they reach the next tree.

Monkeying about
If you let a monkey loose in your room, it would make quite a mess. Monkeys are quick and clever, and take things apart just to see what's inside. They're a lot like people, really.

Not fussy

Fruit and flowers, birds and butterflies, bamboo shoots and crabs, eggs and frogs' legs – most monkeys will eat just about anything.

Capuchin monkey

This monkey lives in South America. It is named after capuchin monks, who wear cloaks that come down in a V-shape over their forehead – just like the brown hairs of a capuchin monkey.

Too big to swing

Most monkeys and apes swing through the treetops. But the biggest kinds move around on the ground on all fours.

Hands for gripping

Monkeys have long, strong fingers and toes. These end in nails, which don't get in the way when the monkey wraps its fingers around a branch or a banana.

Living together

Like people, monkeys live together. Some live in families, but other monkey societies are much bigger, with fifty or more monkeys playing, sleeping, arguing, and eating together.

Golden monkey
In the bamboo forests of China, golden monkeys live in groups, or "troops," of more than one hundred.

Look down! It's a snake!
Vervets let out different shrieks when they spot different kinds of enemies. The "eagle" alarm makes them all look up. When they hear the "leopard" alarm, they go straight up the closest tree.

Young vervet

Twisted tails
The titi monkey family rests cuddled together on a branch. When they go to sleep, they twine their tails together too.

Cleaning up your act
Many monkeys spend hours grooming – picking bugs and dirt out of each other's fur. Grooming also seems to help monkeys get along with each other.

Mother and daughter

Young monkeys stay with their mothers for a long time. This vervet monkey is two years old, but she still sticks close to Mom's side.

Mother vervet

Just like us, monkeys make faces when they're playing

You're the boss

With his tail in the air and a grin on his face, one baboon shows the sole of his foot to another. This is a strange, baboony way of saying – I admit it, you're the boss!

Leaders of the pack

In the baboon world, males are twice the size of females. Some males live on the edges of the troop, while the most important males live in the thick of the pack, surrounded by females and babies.

Funny faces

Some monkeys have the strangest looks on their faces. The cotton-top tamarin (far right) even has a hairstyle to match.

Cotton-top
This little monkey is only the size of a squirrel. It eats nuts like a squirrel, but also feeds on fruit and insects.

Looking good
An unhealthy uakari has a pale pink face. When it is feeling well, the uakari's face turns bright red (but it doesn't get any prettier).

Who knows?
The word *proboscis* means "nose." Any idea why they call it the proboscis monkey?

King of the mustaches
The emperor tamarin (left) flashes its impressive mustache at enemies, trying to appear much bigger than it really is.

Painted face
Young mandrills have dull brown faces. But when the males become adults, they get brilliant red and blue noses.

High flyer
The douc (DOOK) is one of the most agile – and beautiful – monkeys of all. With great shouts and leaps, it can throw itself 20 feet from one tree to the next. No wonder its hair stands on end!

Rare beauty
The golden marmoset has a mane like a lion. Sadly, so many have been caught and sold as pets that there are very few of them left in the wild.

Wild boy of the woods

 Orangutans live in the rain forests of Indonesia and Malaysia. With their shaggy orange fur, huge arms, and pot bellies, you can see how they got their name – which is Malaysian for "wild man of the woods."

Endangered ape
Humans are the orangutan's worst enemy. So much of the rain forest has been cut down that zoos may soon be the only places to find orangs.

Stay out of my (hic) garden
To keep other orangs out of its territory, the male orangutan lets out a booming call – which ends with a series of burps and sighs.

Four hands, no feet
The orangutan's big toes work like thumbs. Its feet are so good at grasping that it seems to have four hands and no feet.

My dad's bigger than your dad
Male orangutans weigh up to 265 pounds – more than the average dad! And they're much better at hanging around in trees, too.

Fruit lover
Ripe fruit is an orangutan's favorite food. When it finds a tree full of figs or mangoes, it picks the juiciest ones and peels them carefully with its enormous fingers.

*Hook-shaped hands,
just right for
hanging on*

Still growing
This male orangutan
is five years old. He won't
leave his mother's side until he's
seven, and won't reach his full
size until he is
twelve.

Where did that branch go?
By the time they've grown
up, one orang in three has
broken a bone by
falling out of a tree!

*An adult male's
arms may stretch
8 feet*

*The fifth toe is
shorter, to make it
easier to swing
through trees*

15

Growing up

A baby gibbon spends its first years clinging to its mother's fur. It has to hang on tight, because she moves fast, and the jungle floor is a long way down.

Living bridge

A baby spider monkey has problems crossing big gaps between two trees. The mother helps out by stretching her body into a living bridge which the little one can scramble across.

Tightrope champ

The gibbon is famous for its tightrope walking. A mother will run gracefully along a branch, with her long arms out for balance and her baby clinging tight to her belly.

Piggyback

When they get a bit older, young monkeys and apes start riding around on Mom's (or even Dad's) back. Soon they will start to spend more time away from her side.

Mother's milk

Like a human, a monkey baby starts drinking its mother's milk from the day it's born. For the first few months it rarely leaves the breast, where a nipple is always close by.

Warning! Fragile

Their mothers are dull gray, but baby leaf monkeys are a bright apricot color. This bold coloring makes older monkeys treat the babies with extra special care.

Playing house

A young chimp spends hours "helping" and copying its mother as she builds a nest for the night. When it finally has to make its own nest, it has a pretty good idea of what to do.

Busy parents
A baby gibbon is born
to a gibbon couple
every two or
three years. It
won't leave
home until
it's eight
years old.

*This baby
gibbon is only
one month old*

Amazing grace

Monkeys are the acrobats of the animal world. They are fast and graceful, and make bounding through the trees look as easy as walking down the street.

King of the swingers

The agile gibbon swings along beneath the branches, hanging on with hands like muscular hooks.

Can monkeys fly?

No primate gets around by flying, gliding, hopping, or digging. But a few, like the proboscis monkey, can dive into the water and swim away from danger.

... and a tail makes five

Using its strong tail like an extra arm, the spider monkey can hang from a branch and still have two hands for eating.

Chimp in space

One of the first apes in space was Ham the chimpanzee. He spent 16 minutes spinning above the Earth at nearly 5,000 miles per hour – wearing a special pressurized chimp suit, of course.

Knuckle walkers

Gorillas and chimpanzees walk on all fours. They plunk their feet flat on the ground, but curl their fingers over and walk on the knuckles of their hands.

Black spider monkey

Stretched out between jungle branches, this Brazilian monkey looks like a huge, hairy spider.

Index

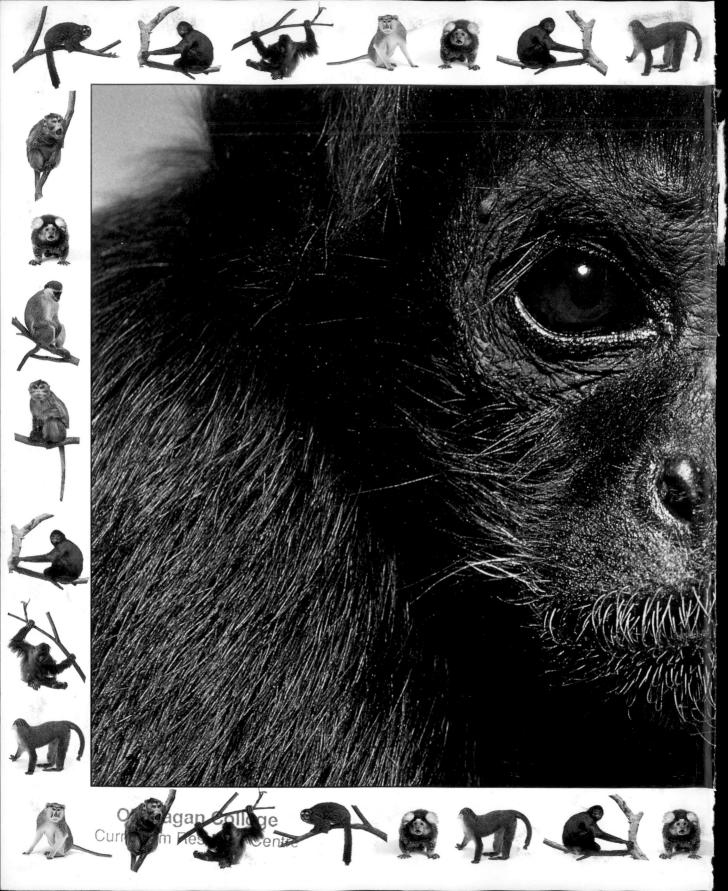